Are They Faking?

A Look at Malingering
Incompetency to Stand Trial (IST)

Victoria Hargan
Masters of Arts Forensic Psychology

Table of Contents

Overview   3

Chapter One
What is Malingering?   4

Chapter Two
Commonly Feigned Disorders and Conditions   16

Chapter Three
Legal Landmark Cases Regarding Competency   24

Chapter Four
Incompetency to Stand Trial   26

Chapter Five
The Forensic Evaluation   33

Chapter Six
Measures of Competency   37

Chapter Seven
Ethical Issues, Considerations in Malingering   50

Chapter Eight
Bioethical Principles in Assessing Malingering   55

Chapter Nine
Gaps in Research and Differential Diagnosis   59

Chapter Ten
Summarizing the Detection of Malingering IST   63

Resources   65

Overview

Competency to stand trial is the most commonly referred
legal question that is referred to forensic psychologists;
making CST-Competency to Stand Trial the most evaluated
of all referrals. This book examines competency to stand
trial as it relates to defendant's who malinger Incompetency
to Stand Trial (IST). The author explores the concept of
Incompetency to stand trial in addition to a variety of
psychological tests utilized by forensic evaluators such as
the Clinical Interview, SIMS; SIRS; MMPI-2; TOMM;
ILK; ECT-R; CST; CAI; to determine malingering
incompetency to stand trial. Motivation behind
malingering, detecting malingering, and malingered crime
related amnesia are also discussed. Themes and patterns
seen in malingering are reviewed. Ethical implications
regarding IST are also explored.

4

Chapter One
What is Malingering?

Incompetency to stand trial is the most common and most assessed of all legal referrals; yet it can also be the most difficult to ascertain among forensic evaluations. "Approximately 60,000 individuals undergo competency to stand trial evaluations annually in the United States" (Pirelli et al, 2011).

What is Malingering? According to the DSM-IV-TR malingering is defined as "the intentional production of false evidence or grossly exaggerated physical or psychological symptoms, motivated by external incentives such as avoiding military duty, avoiding work, obtaining financial compensation, evading criminal prosecution, or obtaining drugs" (DSM-IV-TR pg. 739, 2000). Individuals may malinger in an attempt to avoid pain, or to seek or obtain something for personal advantage or benefit. In some cases, offenders will malinger in an attempt to avoid the death penalty. In Ford v. Wainwright (1989) The Supreme Court held that the execution of insane individuals is unconstitutional. The legal definition of insanity and the medical diagnosis of mental illness or mental retardation is not the same. Having a mental illness or mental retardation does not always determine whether a person is competent to stand trial. This will be discussed later on in this book.

Some other examples of malingering may include avoiding arrest, criminal prosecution or to obtain medications or workman's compensation. The DSM-IV – TR states that "Malingering should be suspected if any of the combination of the following criteria is exhibited:

1.   Medicolegal context of presentation (e.g. the person is referred by an attorney to the clinician for examination).

2.   Marked discrepancy between the claimed stress or disability and the objective findings.

3.   Lack of cooperation during the diagnostic evaluation and in complying with the prescribed treatment regimen.

4.   The presence of Antisocial Personality Disorder" (DSM-IV-TR, 2000).

An Example of Potential Malingering

Here is an example of an offender potentially malingering in an attempt to avoid prosecution due to a psychomedical condition, traumatic brain injury; or TBI; and the offender is feigning (faking) amnesia. The offender is referred to a clinician for evaluation and they claim they do not have any memory of the crime they recently committed. The offender states that they were in a car accident one year ago and suffered a TBI and that is why they cannot remember their crime.

First of all, the offender should be able to back up their claim of having a past history of TBI. This may be in the form of documentation and third party statements to back up the claim of TBI. For example, the clinician should be able to retrieve police reports and medical records for the day of the accident. Additionally, other documentation may include follow up medical visits or rehabilitation pertaining to the brain injury. Malingerers will not be able to back up their claims in most cases.

A Case Study

Alternatively, in some cases person's in car accidents will not always seek medical attention; thus resulting in a lack of documentation and lack of appropriate care for the person who suffered injuries in the car accident. In a Michigan case, an 18 year old female we'll call KP, a habitual alcohol driving related offender was unaware of a TBI that she was suffering from as a result of a car accident two years previous. After KP received five Minor in Possessions (MIP) convictions; 2 alcohol driving related offences; in addition to being arrested on warrants for not appearing for court dates; and violating her probation for showing up at probation appointments on the wrong days; KP confided in her friend for help. He friend's mother was a forensic psychologist. KP's frie asked her mother to help her friend out.

After learning that KP did not have any money for services because she lost her father to an overdose of drugs and alcohol two years previous; she lost her brother to suicide and her mother to cancer one year previous to her convictions. Further, KP was in a car accident just six month after her mother passed away. The car accident forced her head through the side window of her car, shattering the window. Dazed and confused from both the car accident and still grieving from the losses of her mother, her father and her brother sent KP into a downward spiral of alcohol abuse. The accident was reported, but KP refused medical attention. This is not uncommon for victims of car accident's to refuse medical attention.

In some cases, victims do not have health insurance. In other instances, the person is in shock from the car accident and they are not thinking clearly. Another explanation why a person may not seek medical care after a car accident may be due to the physiological response which occurs under traumatic stress. For example, when a person is involved in a car accident, a series of events occur within the body. The brain responds to the perceived threat and a series of physiological events follow, called the fight or flight response. Your body responds with an increased heart rate and blood pressure; the digestive process slows down; blood flow increases to your major muscles; and an increase in adrenaline and cortisol will occur. Cortisol, also known as the stress hormone is produced by the adrenal glands and causes the body to undergo many changes such as lower sensitivity to pain. It is this very response that is responsible for many car accident survivors to ignore care. The adrenaline and cortisol surge in the body increases the endorphins in the body, acting like a natural pain killer. It isn't until the stress response decreases that the accident victim will notice pain and other issues resulting from the car accident. This may be why KP did not seek medical care after the accident. Additionally, KP did not have adequate support systems in her life to help her make vital decisions in her life. In fact, since the age of 16, KP was a caregiver to her 80 year old grandmother since the passing of her mother.

KP's assessment by the forensic psychologist revealed that she had been suffering from posttraumatic stress disorder (PTSD) from the losses of her family members. The car accident exacerbated her PTSD symptoms, in addition to suffering from an untreated head injury. The forensic evaluator submitted her findings to the court. The court took KP's unique circumstance into consideration and referred her to the appropriate resources instead of sentencing her to incarceration.

Sharing this case study was to reveal potential reasons why someone may not have appropriate documentation. Although KP did not have any medical documentation because her injury went untreated, she did however have the police accident report. It is not uncommon for individuals who chase law suits to feign PTSD, TBI or whiplash from a car accident since these conditions are among the most commonly reported injuries to accident victims.

In the initial example of someone feigning TBI and report that they don't remember committing the crime is highly unlikely to exhibit absolute total amnesia after committing a crime; unless they are suffering from crime related amnesia, which will be discussed further on in this book. In addition to crime related amnesia, other conditions such as Dissociative Identity Disorder (DID) may be responsible for an offender having absolutely no memory of committing the crime for which they are charged. These conditions, in addition to the possibility of malingering will be ruled out during a forensic evaluation.

The motivation behind Malingering Incompetency to Stand Trial may be suspected by defendants if they are declaring a diminished capacity defense, to gain sympathy or privileges; or if they prefer psychiatric commitment versus prison. Malingering psychological symptoms has become big business in civil cases and the disability industry. It is not uncommon for someone to feign physiological and psychological symptoms for some sort of gain, such as a law suit. As mentioned in the above example, a client may have a car accident and claim that they are suffering from both whiplash and PTSD as a result of the car accident; when in actuality the client does not possess either condition and continues to feign symptoms in an attempt to win monetary benefits from a law suit.

Malingering is also seen in criminal cases where a defendant is charged with a crime and appears incompetent to stand trial. There must be a bonafide doubt of whether the defendant is competent to stand trial and it is suggested that the threshold for determining a "bonafide doubt" is not very high.

Malingered crime-related amnesia

Malingered crime-related amnesia is a symptom that is claimed by the defendant after they have committed a crime. The motivation for malingering amnesia following a crime is to show that the defendant has no memory of the act; therefore s/he cannot defend themselves. It is not uncommon for defendants of crimes to claim that they do not remember committing the crime in an attempt to avoid arrest or incarceration or other punishment. "Additionally, it is suggested that there are some authentic cases of crime related amnesia due to crime-related stress causing genuine posttraumatic amnesia for the crime; however it is unknown of how many are feigned" (Giger, 2010). For example, an offender may have participated in an armed robbery that ended up in murdering the victim. The offender's partner in crime decided to dismember the victim and dispose of the body. The crime itself was both traumatic and heinous and the offender may initially suffer from trauma related amnesia as a means to protect themselves psychologically. The offender may appear incoherent and in shock. This is an example of why an offender may exhibit crime-related amnesia.

Themes and Patterns in Malingering

Inconsistencies, exaggerations, a history of contradicting statements, and repeating statements are found as common themes among malingerers. For example a client may make several inconsistent and negative self-statements alluding to incompetency as evidenced by his statements of "being incompetent to work; stating that people call him/her crazy; repeatedly states s/he does not remember committing the crime; states that they suffer from blackouts; repeatedly states that they do not recall the crime after every question; makes claims of unstable work history are examples. Other themes or patterns include lack of evidence to support the offenders/litigants claims; such as medical reports, hospitalizations for psychiatric treatment, or witnesses.

Other inconsistencies such as multi-system or multi organ symptomology may be a potential indicator for malingering; however somatoform and factitious disorders should be ruled out. For example when the clinician asks about medical or mental health history or symptoms, the client may pick conditions from several areas that have no connection to one another; such as panic attacks, kidney disease, stating that s/he sees things, forgetfulness are examples; however the client will not be able to back up these claims. Moreover, third party information and reviewing medical, legal, mental health, school, and work history is paramount when corroborating evidence to either accept or reject claims made by the defendant.

Themes observed in the literature include inconsistency while making statements and recanting statements. For example a client may state that they were expelled from school at the beginning of the interview and then later state that they dropped out of school. This is an important finding since both acts could potentially lead to a more accurate diagnosis. For example, it is not uncommon for someone with a conduct disorder to be expelled from school for aggressive or harmful behavior. It is important to find out why the offender was expelled from school. Individual with conduct disorders will exhibit aggressive or harmful behaviors, damages or destroys property (e.g. Vandalism or setting fire), lying and theft (shop lifting or breaking and entering) are examples, truancy and other serious violations, early substance abuse (tobacco, alcohol or drug use), and early sexual activity. Conduct disorders often lead to an adult diagnosis of Antisocial Personality Disorder (ASPD). Being expelled for fighting, or other rule breaking act will reveal past behaviors and school history. Depending on the type of assessment being performed, both are important in the assessment and diagnoses of individuals.

It is important to confront the client on the inconsistency of whether they were either expelled or dropped out of school. The examiner may find that both occurred at some point in the offender's school history.

There are a number of reasons why a person may have been expelled or dropped out. In the above case study, KP dropped out of school to care for her elderly grandmother, and later went on to graduate from an alternative school. Malingerers will most likely confuse the examiner by telling one lie after another. This is why corroborating evidence is so important. The forensic examiner should obtain the offender's school history.

Patterns of a deceptive personality will typically emerge during the evaluation. Deception is common among malingers and those with ASPD. Deceptive behaviors such as lying to the clinician are common; in addition to learning about previous offender convictions that are categorized as deceptive acts like "Larceny by deception" aka; "Larceny by trick" are also common. Larceny by trick is when an individual steals property from another person by deception. For example, the perpetrator who is working as a construction contractor comes to a person's home to put a bid on a roof. The perpetrator will convince the homeowner to give them a substantial check "for supplies" before they begin the job, however the contractor never returns to do the job. These individuals often do this over and over as a way of living until they are caught.

An additional suspicion of malingering is a forthcoming demeanor regarding mental illness or substance abuse in an attempt to appear incompetent. For example, the offender will constantly reinforce that they are mental ill by using frequent statements regarding their mental health and interject them throughout the interview even when the interviewer hasn't asked about it. Additionally, during the interview process the client may exaggerate hallucinations or appear to have a mental illness by speaking incoherently as seen as "word salad" in schizophrenia; or stating things that make the client appear as if they are delusional. To the lay person the offender may convince others that they are mentally ill; but for the trained clinician this is less likely.

Chapter Two
Commonly Feigned Disorders

Feigning or "faking it" can be done in any number of ways; Malingering or "faking it" can be difficult to detect. Commonly feigned conditions or disorders may include:

Feigning Neurological Disorders and Cognitive Impairment

Feigned neurological and cognitive disorders may include: traumatic brain injury, Alzheimer's, dementia, or head injury; mental retardation; learning disability; autism; brain injury or other cognitive deficit disorder (Oorsouw & Merkelbach, 2010). Defendants who feign neurological impairment will typically present with atypical neurologic symptoms or illogical or inconsistent symptoms of a given disorder (Widows et al., 2007). For example the offender may state that they have brain injury as a result of an accident they had last year. They may state that their symptoms include memory loss, problems concentrating, and stomach ache. The symptom of stomach ache may be that the offender has a stomach ache as result of the stress of the arrest or some other issue like the flu. There will be no evidence of brain injury after conducting a CAT scan, and EEG-electroencephalogram, or other psychological testing. In fact if an offender is malingering "The respondent's score on the Neurologic Impairment scale will be significantly elevated above the recommended cutoff score for the identification of feigned or exaggerated neurologic symptoms" (Widows et al, 2007). It should be noted that there are many cases where Traumatic Brain Injury (TBI) symptoms are not detected on imaging; thus making both the diagnosis of TBI and the potential for malingering challenging for the medical and mental health professions.

Feigning Psychiatric Disorders

Feigning Psychosis, Schizophrenia, Bi-polar, Posttraumatic Stress Disorder, and Delusional Disorder are other common conditions feigned by defendants. Defendants who feign psychiatric disorders may do so to appear "Incompetent" by exhibiting both objective and subjective symptoms. For example a client may state that they hear voices. This is a subjective complaint.

Subjective complaints are those that are self-reported by the client and are not a tangible symptom that can be seen. The client may begin talking back to the voices, mumbling and speaking incoherently. This is an *objective symptom* that is observed by the clinician. However determining the validity of the voices should be determined through a battery of psychological tests, interviews and collateral evidence. The Structured Inventory of Malingering Symptomology (SIMS) psychological instrument provides that "The Psychosis scale reflects the degree to which a respondent endorses unusual psychotic symptoms that are not typically present in actual psychiatric patients. Such a presentation includes symptoms that are illogical or bizarre, that vary in extremity or course from documented symptoms of psychosis, or that occur very rarely" (Widow et al., 2007).

Feigning Hallucinations

When a defendant claims that they are exhibiting hallucinations it is important for the clinician to ask detailed questions about the hallucinations. Hallucinations are frequently related to a delusion 88% of the time. Additionally, "In schizophrenia, the major themes are persecutory or instructive" (Resnik & Knoll, 2005).

Determining the validity of command auditory hallucinations may be challenging to the forensic examiner; in addition these types of hallucinations can be easily feigned. "Individuals who experience true command hallucinations do not always obey the voices, especially if doing so would be dangerous and are typically present with non-command hallucinations" (Resnik & Knoll, 2005).

Furthermore, command hallucinations typically do not happen only once and without psychotic features. The clinician should be suspect to malingering if the evaluee states that the only time they had ever experienced an auditory command hallucination was at the time of the offense. "Genuine schizophrenic hallucinations tend to diminish when patients are involved in activities and will typically cope by engaging in activities such as socializing, working, listening to a radio, watching TV, lying down, walking and taking medications" (Resnik & Knoll, 2005).

If a clinician suspects a defendant of malingering auditory hallucinations they should ask the defendant what they do to make the voices go away. Patients who are not feigning can typically stop the auditory hallucinations either by activity, medications or remission; and a malingerer would not be aware of this (Resnik & Knoll, 2005). Malingerers will offer an unusual description of the auditory hallucination such as stating "the voice told me to commit rape" or, "a bank robber who claims that voices kept screaming "Stick up, stick up, stick up!" (Resnik & Knoll, 2005). "Furthermore, visual hallucinations are experienced by an estimated 24% to 30% of psychotic individuals but are reported much more often by malingerers (46%) than by persons with genuine psychosis" (4%)" (Resnik & Knoll, 2005).

Feigning Psychopathy

According to the DSM-IV-TR "Antisocial Personality Disorder is a pervasive pattern of disregard for, and violation of, the rights of others that begins in childhood or early adolescence and continues into adulthood" (pg. 701, 2000). "This pattern has also been referred to as Psychopathy, sociopathy, or dissocial personality disorder; because deceit and manipulation are central features of Antisocial Personality Disorder" DSM-IV-TR 2000). "APD is characterized by a pervasive pattern of disregard for the rights of others as evidenced by at least three of the following criteria: repeatedly engaging in illegal behavior; frequently lying, using aliases or conning others for personal profit; impulsivity and lack of future planning; irritability and aggressiveness; reckless disregard for the safety of self and others; consistent irresponsibility, with repeated failures to sustain employment or fulfill financial obligations; lack of remorse as evident in indifference to or rationalization of hurting, mistreating or stealing from others" (DSM-IV-TR 2000).

It is interesting to note that deception is a key trait in Psychopathy and it is suggested that Psychopathy and malingering are associated as a result of the manipulative, lying, and ability to con individuals for personal profit or gain. Malingering has these same traits. According to the DSM-IV, if a client is diagnosed with Antisocial Personality Disorder, then malingering should be considered (DSM-IV, 2000).

Feigning Low Intelligence

Low IQ, learning disability, mental retardation, cognitive deficit disorders are also claimed by malingerers. "The Low Intelligence scale reflects the degree to which a respondent endorses cognitive incapacity or intellectual deficits that are inconsistent with capacities and knowledge typically present in individuals with cognitive or intellectual deficits. Such a presentation includes providing incorrect responses to very simple items or providing approximate answers.

The respondent's score on the Low Intelligence scale is significantly elevated above the recommended cutoff score for the identification of feigned or exaggerated cognitive incapacity or low intellect" (Widow et al, 2007). In Atkins v. Virginia (2002), The Supreme Court declared that the execution of mentally retarded individuals as unconstitutional.

Feigning Amnesia

Other conditions that may be feigned may include Amnesic disorder related to general medical condition; medication or long term substance use/abuse; Dissociative Amnesia; Dissociative Fugue; Dissociative Identity Disorder, Brain Injury, and substance use disorder (Widows et al). According to Widows *"The Amnestic Disorders scale reflects the degree to which a respondent's symptoms support memory impairment that is inconsistent with the patterns typically seen in impairment seen in brain dysfunction or injury. This type of presentation supports symptoms that differ from those experienced by brain-injured patients in terms of onset, course, or nature, and generally reflects an unsophisticated knowledge of a true amnestic disorder. The respondent's score on the Amnestic Disorders scale is significantly elevated above the recommended cutoff score for the identification of feigned or exaggerated amnestic symptoms"* (Widow et al., 2007).

According to Granhag & Stromwall "Homicide offenders who claim "amnesia" (memory loss) for their crime is very common to avoid punishment. It is also stated that 25-40% of those found guilty of homicide feign amnesia" (Schacter, 1986; Taylor and Kopelman, 1984). Finally, many offenders will feign a variety of symptoms all at once that are not at all related to see which one may catch the attention of the evaluator.

Chapter Three

Legal Landmark Cases Regarding Competency

Dusky v. United States: Two Prongs

An incompetency to stand trial evaluation requires that the forensic evaluator finds an absence of either one of or both of the two prongs, stated in Dusky v. United States. Dusky v. the United States is the landmark case notable for incompetency to stand trial. "The Supreme Court set forth a definition of competency to stand trial that has since come to be the standard in federal court and most state jurisdictions" (Melton et al, 2007). "The court stated that the test must be whether the defendant has sufficient present ability to consult with his attorney with a reasonable degree of rational understanding and a rational as well as factual understanding of the proceedings against him" (Melton et al., 2007).

The Two Prongs to the competency test include:

1. Ability to have a rational and factual understanding of the charges against them.(Melton et al, 2007)

2. And ability to collaborate with their attorney and formatting a defense strategy. (Melton et al., 2007).

In addition to Dusky v US there are four additional landmark cases that have impacted how incompetency to stand trial is determined.

1. **In Wilson v US**-ruled that amnesia or memory loss is not an automatic bar for incompetency to stand trial. (Elkins 2011).

2. **In Jackson v Mississippi** the defendant cannot be held indefinitely in a psychiatric institution; and only for a reasonable amount of time. Each jurisdiction varies; however it is typically six months in most jurisdictions. (Elkins 2011).

3. **In Drope v Missouri 1975** ruled that there should be a bonafide doubt of CST to be raised; and should not be used as a strategic tactic to find out information about the defendant. It is suggested that the threshold is not very high and having a mental illness can prompt a competency to stand trial evaluation. (Elkins, 2010).

4. **Finally, in Riggnis v Nevada (1992)** ruled that "a defendant is not incompetent to stand trial simply because he takes prescribed psychotropic drugs or other medication without which he might be deemed incompetent to stand trial" (Elkins, 2010).

Chapter Four

Incompetency to Stand Trial

Incompetency to stand trial may result due to a mental disease or mental defect as a result of a traumatic or genetic condition; mental illness; mental retardation, IQ, developmental disability, developmental age and stage of the defendant, maturity, mental health of the defendant, or brain injury, that may render them incapable to understand the charges against them; and the ability to assist in their defense.

Other potential factors resulting in incompetency to stand trial include the potential for malingering. Competency to stand trial serves many purposes. "It serves to safeguard the accuracy of criminal adjudications, to guarantee a fair trial, preserve the dignity and integrity of legal processes, and to ensure that the defendant knows why he is being punished if he is found guilty" (Felthous, pg. 19, 2011).

Competency to stand trial has many tentacles and any one of them a potential ethical, legal violation or issue. For example, if the defendant is truly malingering and the forensic examiner failed to detect it; the defendant would be found incompetent to stand trial. The malingerer may be subjected to unnecessary antipsychotic medications;

causing harm to them. Some antipsychotics have serious permanent side effects; such as tardive dyskinesia.

On the other hand, if the defendant is found competent to stand trial and thought to be "malingering" this too can have devastating consequences. The defendant will not receive the proper treatment or care they need; including medications. The defendant would not only be subjected to harsher punishment, but to a potentially dangerous environment if incarcerated versus being institutionalized. Individuals with brain injury, brain impairment, mental retardation, or mental illness are already a vulnerable population. High stress and volatile environments such as prison may exacerbate their symptoms.

Additionally, this finding may potentially violate the defendants "right to treatment" if the original forensic examiner finds the defendant to be feigning or malingering. For example if the client is found to be competent to stand trial and the forensic examiner's professional opinion states that the offender is "faking it" or malingering, then the offender may be viewed as faking a real mental illness. Once under the authority of prison officials, it is often difficult to receive the appropriate care. It is not uncommon for mental illness to go undetected for many years, or in some cases a life time. This is particularly true of young adult offenders who have never been diagnosed with a mental illness; however they may have been exhibiting mental illness symptoms prior to the onset of the crime. Since the typical age of onset for male schizophrenics is in the early twenties, the offender may not yet have been diagnosed. This may be true if the offender and the offender's parents noticed symptoms, but rationalized it as something else such as stress, moody teenager, and substance abuse. Unless a person is aware of signs or symptoms of a mental illness, it would be easy to chalk it off to something else. In fact, in 2006 "a study by the U.S. Department of Justice's Bureau of Justice Statistics (BJS) showing that 64 percent of local jail inmates, 56 percent of state prisoners and 45 percent of federal prisoners have symptoms of serious mental illnesses is an indictment of the nation's mental healthcare system" (Fitzpatrick, 2006).

It should also be noted that there is a high rate of PTSD in prisons/jails after incarceration. This has also been called Post Incarceration Syndrome (PICS) and many do not have the condition until they have been incarcerated. It is suggested that the development of PTSD after incarceration comes from a variety of factors. The most obvious and initial cause is the shock of having your freedom and liberties taken away, in addition to the harsh prison environment where inmates are immediately put on high alert for their own safety. Virtually all inmates develop a high sense of hyper-vigilance and this high level of stress can eventually change brain chemistry, causing the many symptoms of PTSD. Conversely, the development of PTSD in prison is a result of other variables including prolonged incarceration, having few opportunities for rehabilitation, job training and education enhancement. However it the more severe symptoms such as prisoners who are subjected to prolonged solitary confinement and severe institutional abuse, similar to that of prisoners of war in a war setting that have a significant impact on the inmate.

According to Gorski "The severity of symptoms is related to the level of coping skills prior to incarceration, the length of incarceration, the restrictiveness of the incarceration environment, the number and severity of institutional episodes of abuse, the number and duration of episodes of solitary confinement, and the degree of involvement in educational, vocational, and rehabilitation programs" (2001), will all have an impact on whether or not the inmate will develop either PTSD or PICS.

Competency to Stand Trial (CST) is a delicate issue and the opinion of a forensic evaluator is taken very seriously by the judge and jury. There will always be someone who will attempt to malinger in an attempt to avoid punishment or for some other personal gain. However, it is the forensic examiners job to meticulously assess each client as individually and unique to their overall circumstances and biopsychosocial makeup. Further, forensic examiners must be cognizant in their objectivity and careful not to "generalize, or stigmatize" the mentally ill. Just because a defendant has a mental illness or is taking a psychotropic drug does not automatically indicate that someone is incompetent to stand trial. The forensic examiner could be found in violation of being "impartial or bias" if doing so.

According to the specialty guidelines for forensic psychologists "When offering expert opinion to be relied upon by a decision maker, teaching , or conducting research, the forensic psychologist embraces nonpartisanship and demonstrates commitment to the goals of accuracy, objectivity, fairness, and independence. The forensic psychologist treats all participants and weighs all data, opinions and rival hypothesis impartially" (APA, 1991).

The forensic examiner has a considerable amount of responsibility when assessing malingering incompetency to stand trial. The court relies on the forensic examiner to determine the presence or absence of malingering, determination of competency; and the likelihood of competency restoration through evaluation and asking for their opinion.

If a client is found incompetent to stand trial, the protocol is to hospitalize the client until competency is restored; this will vary according to the client's condition. Many times the courts will order a six month review of the client's condition at which point an additional evaluation will be performed. This is a good time for the forensic examiner to read the defendants records for signs of feigning. This can be done by talking to the staff and reviewing medical records to determine if there are any consistencies or inconsistencies in their overall presentation. For example a client may present with feigning a lack of understanding or present with symptoms of psychosis or other psychiatric symptom while they are with staff. On the other hand, when they are socializing with other patients they will not present with this lack of understanding or other symptoms that they may be feigning.

In order to prevent any legal ramifications from either side and for the protection of the forensic evaluator, the forensic evaluator must document any inconsistency, in addition to other third party observations such as observations made by the staff.

It should be noted that an incompetency to stand trial decision is not a "get out of jail free card"; nor is it a way to avoid taking responsibility for the defendant's actions. However the defendant may believe it is; and may not realize that malingering can be detected through an integrated approach; including the use of psychological instruments. The death penalty would be the ultimate injustice to someone who is found competent to stand trial that is truly incompetent to stand trial. Some individuals are very good at feigning, while others are not.

Chapter Five
The Forensic Evaluation

The Clinical Interview

The clinical interview is the single most important step in the detection of malingering IST. A clinical interview can provide the clinician with a wealth of information about the client simply by observing and assessing both verbal and non-verbal cues to deception. The interview is where the clinician will ask the defendant questions related to competency to stand trial and will have the opportunity look for cues of exaggeration, fabrication; and inconsistently.

In addition the clinician will assess the mental status of the client (MSE). The clinical interview actually consists of many other interviews. For example, the initial step of the clinical interview is an intake; therefore an intake interview will take place. The clinician will inform the evaluee of the upcoming tests and procedures that will take place, in addition to the role that the clinician will engage. This is also known as the orientation interview. The clinician is orienting the evaluee to the upcoming procedures and tests. Finally, observing behaviors can be a strong indicator in the detection of deception, and to the current mental state of the evaluee; this is also known as the observational interview (John Jay School of Criminal Justice, 2011).

The clinical interview will set the tone for establishing the evaluee's credibility. The clinician be aware of patterns of inconsistency and should listen carefully to the defendant's account of how they felt (e.g. emotions, thoughts and behaviors) just before the offense, during the offence and after the offense. This will set the basis for both the evaluation. It is important to determine what took place before the offense; also known as preparatory actions. For example, the client may have bought duct tape, a gun and rope prior to the offense. This would indicate the client's motivation in addition to the client's competency to think the crime through by way of planning the crime before actually committing the crime.

Although these questions may be similar to questions relating to Not Guilty by Reason of Insanity, they are posed to see if the defendant can rationally and relevantly communicate with his/her attorney in order to prepare their case.

Additionally asking about events regarding before, during and after the offense may be asked to evaluate whether the defendant is indeed telling the truth. For example, the defendant may say he doesn't remember committing the crime and further into the interview mentions many things that occurred during the crime. This is an inconsistency that should be further investigated.

It is important for the clinician to allow the defendant to talk without interrupting to provide for a more detail account from the defendant's perspective. It is important to listen to the defendant's responses carefully as they may actually tell you they were feeling just after they told you they don't remember committing the crime. This would be considered an inconsistency and a suspicion for malingering. These questions will assist in identifying the capacity to disclose information to the defendant's attorney.

Another factor in determining competency to stand trial is whether or not the defendant has the Capacity to Testify Relevancy. Therefore, it is vital for the clinician to evaluate the defendant's ability to verbally communicate and is relevant to the case during the trial.

The clinical interview is where most of the verbal communication will take place, including asking questions to the defendant to determine Competency to Stand Trial. Depending on the type of assessment used the clinical interview will be where the client will answer questions related to competency; for example the CAI instrument consists of 13 factors related to competency that may be asked during the interview.

Chapter Six

Measures of Competency

Measuring competency involves three main factors:

- Understanding: factual understand of proceedings
- Reasoning: Ability to assist counsel
- Appreciation: Rational understanding of the proceeding

Psychological Instruments to Measure Competency

The Competency Screening Test (CST)

The Competency Screening Test (CST) consists of a 22 items that are designed for sentence completion by the evaluee. It is often the first psychological instrument implemented when determining competency to stand trial. "Scoring includes: Scores range from 2 (competent answer) to 0 (incompetent answer) where scores less than 20 suggest possible incompetence to stand trial. Research has found that the CST produces many false positives; for example, defendants' who are actually competent and labeling them incompetent" (Melton et al, 2007).

This instrument is still utilized by some forensic evaluators as their first line of defense in evaluating CST; however the reliability and validity of the CST is questionable; thus making this instrument less valid and used.

CST Examples of sentence structure completion test may include:

- "When I go to court, the lawyer will:"
- " If the jury finds me guilty, I:"
- " While listening to the witnesses testify against me:"
- "When the jury hears my case, they will:"
- "When I go to court the lawyer will:"
- "When they say a man is innocent until proven guilty I:" (Melton et al, 2007).

The Competency Assessment Instrument (CAI)

The CAI is a typically a one hour structured interview that assesses 13 factors related to competency for standing trial. The items included in this instrument include "Appraisal of available legal defenses", quality of relating to the attorney", and "capacity to disclose pertinent facts" (Roesch et al, 2004).

The scoring is determined by a range from 1 (total incapacity) to 5 (total capacity). For example, the Appraisal of the role of the judge, jury, defendant, witness, defense counsel and prosecuting attorney would be addressed to the defendant; and the defendant should be able to identify each role as to what they do or are responsible for. For example the defendant may state that the judge is neutral and the jury decides who is guilty or innocent. "Additionally, research has revealed that the CAI to have 90% agreement with competency decisions made after extensive hospital evaluations" (Oorsouw & Merkelbach 2010). The CAI has been used more as an interview structuring device with the CST.

ECST-R- The Evaluation of Competency to Stand Trial

The ECST-R is a psychological instrument designed to detect both malingering/feigning and competency measures. 'This test provides competency scales derived from the Dusky standard including ability to consult with counsel=6 items; factual understanding of court proceedings= 6 items; and rational understanding of courtroom proceedings=7 items" (Acklin, C., 2000). 'Feigning scales include uses of Atypical Presentation (ATP) scales that are organized by content such as either psychotic or not psychotic and alleged impairment"(Rogers & Johansson-Love, 2009). "In addition the test is rated on a five-point rating scale: 0, not observed; 1, questionable clinical significance; 2, mild impairment unrelated to competency; 3, moderate impairment that will affect but not by itself impair competency; and 4, severe impairment that substantially impairs competency" (Rogers & Johansson & Love, 2009).

ILK-The Inventory of Legal Knowledge

The ILK is a test designed to "detect feigned deficits in legal knowledge" ((Acklin, C, 2011). The ILK (ILK; Musick & Otto, 2010; Otto, Musick, & Sherrod, 2010) is a newer psychologist instrument used to detect malingering Incompetency to stand trial and contains 61 items administered as a structured interview. The ILK is designed for English speaking evaluees who are at least 12 years old and with a reading level of a 5th grader (Rubenzer, 2011). *It is important to note that the ILK is not designed for individuals with cognitive deficits* and the interpreter should include this in the reporting of the results if the defendant does have cognitive limitations. "Moreover, below chance performance results is considered to be solid evidence of feigning regardless of intellectual level." (Rubenzer, 2011).

This psychological instrument tests the defendant's knowledge of legal knowledge; however the authors intended the ILK to be utilized as an instrument to detect malingering IST. The test requires a true or false response from the evaluee and is easy to score. The examiner simply circles the correct answers on the scoring sheet and then tallies the responses from the test at the end for a total number. (Rubenzer, 2011).

Additionally, the ILK can be interpreted two ways. A "Significantly below-chance performance has long been considered the gold standard in psychometric malingering assessment (Berry & Schipper, 2008; Boone, 2007; Slick, Sherman, & Iverson, 1999; Sweet, Condit, & Nelson, 2008), and ILK scores below 24 exceed the 95% confidence interval for chance-level performance. Perhaps as important, data presented in the ILK manual suggest that nearly 50% of actual malingerers obtain scores this low; a much higher percentage than reported for many other instruments relying on this strategy" (Rubenzer, 2011).

Minnesota Multiphasic Personality Inventory-2 (MMPI-2)

The MMPI-2 is the most commonly used psychological instrument among forensic assessment for psychopathology and disability assessments (Burke, 2007). The MMPI-2 is a self-reporting personality measure designed with a true or false response from the evaluee. Some issues regarding The MMPI-2 are determining whether the evaluee has a tendency to exaggerate or minimize their psychological problems. For example they may "fake good" or "fake bad" or simply chose items by random. A defendant may fake bad or feign (malinger) in an attempt to appear not competent, to avoid criminal responsibility, to avoid arrest or prosecution.

On the other hand an evaluee may "fake good" to impress a potential employer, child custody case, or to get into an academic program by presenting an overly positive self-image by checking answers that would be in positive in nature" (Burke, 2007). *The MMPI-2 consists of 567 items which include; 10 clinical scales and seven validity scales.*
The clinical scales include:
Scale 1 Hypochondriasis (Hs),

Scale 2 Depression (D),

Scale 3 Hysteria (Hy),

Scale 4 Psychopathic Deviate (Pd),

Scale 5 Masculinity-Femininity (Mf),

Scale 6 Paranoia (Pa),

Scale 7 Psychasthenia (Pt),

Scale 8 Schizophrenia (Sc),

Scale 9 Hypomania (Ma),

Scale 0 Social Introversion (Si); inconsistency Scale or TRIN (Graham, 1993)" (Burke, 2007).

A study performed by Kucharski, et al revealed that "Criminal defendants with antisocial personality disorder

(APD), those with a personality disorder other than APD (OPD) and those without a personality disorder (NoPD) were compared on validated measures of malingering using the MMPI-2 in addition to other measures" (Kucharski et al, 2006).

Results of the study revealed "the APD group scored significantly higher on the Minnesota Multiphasic Personality Inventory-2(MMPI-2) F, Fp, and F-K scales" (Kucharski et al., 2006).

44

Figure 1

An MMPI-2 Percentage Measure of Exceeded
Cutoff Scores in Participants in three groups;
Antisocial Personality Disorder (APD),
Participants who have Personality Disorders other
than APD (OPD), and Participants who do not
have Personality Disorders (NoPD).

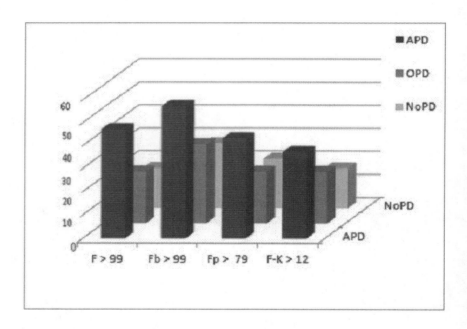

MMPI-2 Scales of Validity

K Scale – "Defensiveness (McKinley, Hathaway &Meehl, 1948). This scale includes 30 items and is a valuable screen for defensiveness. It should be noted that individuals with high education or high socio-economic status may also score high on this scale. (Gordon 2011). "K assumes psychopathology" (Gordon 2011).

F Scale –"Infrequency (Hathaway &McKinley, 1951) "This scale contains 60 items and is a good measure for overall psychopathology. High scores may assume possible random, exaggerated, or mis-scored profile. High scores (>T70), best measure of overall psychopathology, resentment, acting out, moodiness. Mostly elevations in the F scale are due to psychopathology" (Gordon 2011).

Fb –"Back F scale (Butcher, Dahlstrom, Graham & Tellegen, 1989). If Fb is above T999, and F is not high, then the individual may have randomly responded to the latter part of the test. This is more likely than the other possible interpretation, namely that the testee decompensated toward the end of the test" (Gordon 2011).

F(p)- "Infrequency-Psychopathology Scale (Aribisi and Ben-Porath,1995a, 1995b); This scale contains 27 items and The F(p) is better than F or Fb in detecting feigning serious psychopathology" (Gordon 2011).

MacArthur Competence Assessment Tool-(MacCAT-CA)

The MacCAT-CA is composed of 22 items that divided into three scales; 8 items for Factual understanding of proceedings; 8 items and appreciation for ability to assist counsel; and 6 items for Rational Understand of the proceedings (Melton et al, 2007).

SIMS-Structured Inventory of Malingered Symptomology

The SIMS (Widows & Smith, 2004) "The SIMS assesses for the over-reporting of psychiatric and neurocognitive symptoms. It contains 75 items and screens for a wide range of fabricated symptoms. It contains five subscales corresponding to symptom domains that are known to be popular among malingerers: low intelligence, affective disorder, neurological impairment, psychosis, and amnesic disorder" (Oorsouw & Merkelbach, 2010). Oorsouw $ Merkelbach provide examples of items that contain both bizarre and nonexistent symptoms such as: "Sometimes I lose all feeling in my hand so that it is as if I am wearing a glove" and "When I can't remember something, hints don't help". It is suggested that since malingerers tend to exaggerate they will most likely choose answers that are either non-existent or bizarre in nature. Widows states that the SIMS is a good indicator of both Psychopathy and Cognitive impairments (Widows & Smith, 2004).

SIRS-Structured Interview of Reported symptoms

The SIRS (Rogers et al., 1992) is another psychological instrument that is used to measure feigned mental disorders in addition to the over-reporting of psychiatric and neurocognitive symptoms, and both focus on symptom reporting. However, "Unlike the SIMS, the SIRS is a structured interview and has been widely adopted as the gold standard for malingering research on feigned mental disorders in both clinical and forensic practice. It consists of 172 items organized into eight scales" (Oorsouw & Merkelbach, 2010). "The scales include rare and absurd symptoms, blatant and subtle symptoms, unusual symptom combinations, lack of symptom selectivity, extreme symptom severity, and inconsistencies between reported versus observed symptoms. Thus, items are of the type: 'Is the government trying to keep track of your actions? Is it using military aircraft to do this?' and 'Do you become nervous and fidgety whenever you use the bathroom?" Oorsouw & Merkelbach, 2010).

In addition, defensiveness, self-appraisal of honesty and inconsistencies are evaluated and the evaluee will fall into one three categories: feigning, not feigning, or indeterminate. (Oorsouw & Merkelbach, 2010).

Test of Memory Malingering (TOMM)

The TOMM originated by Tombaugh (1996), is a 50 item recognition actuarial instrument used to assess true memory loss of patients who are impaired and individuals who may be malingering. "The initial validation studies of the TOMM indicate that this instrument is a useful test for detecting exaggerated or malingered memory impairment" (Teichner & Wagner, 2004).

Additionally Tombaugh's conducted an investigation on elderly patients whose cognition was intact versus elderly patients who were cognitively impaired. (Teichner & Wagner, 2004). "His investigations revealed correct classification of 95% of all non-demented patients as not malingering. In a separate investigation, Tombaugh assessed the performance of patient controls, cognitively intact controls, and litigating versus non-litigating TBI patients on the TOMM. Results indicated that the litigating TBI group scored significantly lower than the other groups, while the non-litigating TBI patients did not differ from controls. Tombaugh's initial validation studies of the TOMM support the validity and clinical utility of this instrument in detecting cognitive malingering" (Teichner, G., Wagner, 2004).

Chapter Seven
Ethical Issues and Considerations in Malingering

Ethical principles are a fundamental foundation for the psychology and medical professional that must include competency, clarity and objectivity. There are ten potential ethical issues relating to exaggeration and malingering provided by Iverson:

1). *The Failure to produce well-researched effort tests*- It is important for the forensic psychologist to utilize empirically validated tests; otherwise "the accuracy of the conclusion drawn from those tests may be found to be of poor effort or adequate effort";

2*). The forensic psychologist should not utilize effort tests for only defense cases*- If the psychology professional does this, then they are promoting bias, partisanship and violating a fundamental responsibility of impartiality;

3). *"Utilizing more or less effort tests throughout the evaluation.* For example "if the forensic psychologist is retained by either side and only gives one effort test, such as the Test of Memory malingering, during plaintiff evaluations and not examining performance patterns on other tests, such as Digit span. In contrast, for defense evaluations, the clinician might give three effort tests and examine performance" (Iverson, 2006);

4). *"Utilizing different effort tests depending on which side is retained by the forensic psychologist"* (Iverson, 2006). "Using effort tests different depending on which side retains the forensic psychologist" (Iverson, 2006). "For example, the forensic psychologist may provide simple effort tests at the end of the evaluation or after more difficult tests. Researchers have found that this does reduce the sensitivity of the effort test" (Iverson, 2006);

5). *"The forensic psychologist should not warn or "prompt" the client before taking an effort test"* (Iverson, 2006). According to Iverson, it is appropriate to inform patients that there will be tests that detect malingering, poor effort and exaggeration; however it is not appropriate to tell the client which test it is that does this either subtly or blatantly. (Iverson, 2006). This may produce inaccurate results of the tests;

6). *Interpretation of test results should be consistent.* "An ethical issue would arise if the tests were interpreted differently depending on which side the forensic psychologist is retained by" (Iverson, 2006);

7). *The forensic psychologist should not assume that a client put forth their "best effort" because the evaluee simply past the test.* "There are four reasons why this assumption might not be correct" (Iverson, 2006):

- "**First**, passing an effort test simply means the person passed the effort test. It does not mean that the person gave his or her best effort during the neuropsychological evaluation" (Iverson, 2006).It is the responsibility of the forensic psychologist to observe behaviors and performance during the entire evaluation and not only by a single test.

- "**Second**, in nearly every analog malingering study, there is a subset of participants who are deliberately faking deficits during testing but who are not detected with the procedure under study. False-negative rates are often high due to cutoff scores designed to minimize false positives" (Iverson, 2006).

- "**Third**, it is entirely possible that a person chooses not to underperform, or underperforms to a small degree, on that specific test; whereas, on other tests the poor effort might be more prominent" (Iverson, 2006).

- "**Finally**, it is possible that attorney coaching (Youngjohn, 1995) could affect how a patient performs on a specific test (e.g., the MMPI-2 or a

computerized effort test). Some researchers have
reported that coached subjects are less likely to be
accurately identified on effort tests (e.g., DiCarlo et
al., 2000; Frederick & Foster, 1991; Rose, Hall,
Szalda- Petree, & Bach, 1998)" (Iverson, 2006).
8). *"Interpreting effort test failure or exaggerated
symptoms, in isolation, as malingering"* (Iverson,
2006). Effort tests measure exaggeration and whether
the defendant is putting forth effort also known as
detecting poor effort that is seen in malingering.
Malingering is concluded by a multitude of factors;
including observation of behaviors; test interpretation,
motivation of the defendant, potential psychiatric
disturbance, lack of cooperation by the evaluee and the
potential for false positives.

In addition, if the evidence is "too provocative or
derogatory for the forensic psychology's comfort, it
would be appropriate to discuss exaggeration and poor
effort as behavior without making the conclusion of
malingering. The psychologist should list all potential
differential diagnosis or explanations that could
attribute to the evidence" (Iverson, 2006); 9). *The
forensic psychologist should be aware of and to not
intentionally interpret exaggerations as a cry for help;*

10). *The forensic psychologist should be up to date on the latest tests to remain competent, responsible and informed.*

Chapter Eight

Bioethical Principles in Assessing Malingering

Additional ethical issues that should be considered in malingering IST include violating autonomy of the evlauee. *Autonomy* is one of the bioethical principal's that promotes the sense of "self" when making independent, individual choices and decisions regarding their care. In IST the client does not have a choice in deciding whether they want to participate in a competency to stand trial evaluation. This decision is made by the court and out of the hands of the client.

The psychology professional should aid in helping the client attain autonomy by offering honest, clear, detailed information regarding evaluation, care, treatment planning and legal situation. Even though a client may be deemed IST, the mentally ill defendant still has rights; the right to refuse treatment for example. In an incompetent client, a guardian would be appointed to assist in making those decisions.

Additionally, the psychology professional should do all that they can to help the client and the client's guardian in making choices in promoting self-determination; in order to make the best possible decision from all available options. Respecting the client's choice is another way to promote autonomy; regardless of their choice and whether we agree with their choice or decisions (APA 2010). In CST, the defendant does not have control over the CST; the court does. The defendant cannot exercise their right to autonomy if there is a "bonafide doubt" of CST the court will order an evaluation (Melton et al., 2007).

Beneficence is the promotion of good. This principle reinforces promoting actions to clients that will benefit them in making the best decision for them by weighing all available options. The option with the least possible harm should be taken (APA 2010). An example of beneficence in IST is declaring a defendant IST and the court orders the client to take antipsychotic medication to deem them competent. This is also known as "synthetic sanity."

Nonmaleficence *is the bioethical principle* promoting "to do no harm". This is a fundamental principle in psychology. In order to avoid potential ethical conflicts or violations, the forensic psychologist should weigh potential outcomes when evaluating risks versus benefits in each individual client. For example, since the criminal justice system is part of an adversarial arena, there is always going to be one side encouraging an incompetency to stand trial outcome.

On the other side; they will be hoping for a "malingering" outcome. It is essential that the forensic psychologist not get caught up in the partisanship of one side or the other; particularly the hiring client. This would be potentially viewed as "a gun for hire"; or "hired gun". This would not only hurt the client, but the reputation of the forensic psychologist that may also include sanctions from the state board (APA 2010).

Finally, *Justice* is the principle that promotes the moral rightness, fairness, or equity of the client. Although all clients should be treated fairly and just by affording all clients equal opportunity to receive access to potential resources; including medical, mental health services; it does not mean that all clients should receive the same treatment plan. Every individual is unique and should be treated as such (APA 2010).

Chapter Nine
Gaps in Research and Differential Diagnosis

Gaps in research in reference to malingering incompetency to stand trial include malingering that co-occurs in individuals who have a genuine psychosocial problem (Adetunji, et al., 2006). Other gaps in research include differential diagnoses as it relates to malingering. Research has indicated that malingering may be a symptom to another disorder such as factitious disorders, attention seeking disorders, and somatoform disorders.

Symptoms seen in Somatoform Disorders are unconsciously feigned however they are typically motivated by external gain, such as attention, financial compensation or to avoid a stressful situation, include arrest and incarceration. DSM-IV criteria provides "that persons diagnosed with somatization disorder, undifferentiated Somatoform disorder, conversion disorder, pain disorder, hypochondriasis, and body dysmorphic disorder would also not be classified as malingerers" (DSM-IV-TR, 2000).

In addition, ***"Factitious disorders*** also are distinguished from malingering in that there are no external incentives present" (Bordini et al, 2002); and that they are motivated by assuming a sick role. "Moreover, persons with mTBI- Mild Traumatic Brain Injury may exhibit problems with memory, inattention, slow processing, and difficulties with their activities of daily living should not be characterized as exaggeration or malingering in mTBI; since symptoms mimic both conditions"(Bordini et al, 2002).

Since malingering is a diagnosis that is made by exclusion, it is imperative that the clinician rule out general medical conditions that may be responsible for the many symptoms claimed by the evaluee and corroborate collateral evidence, documents such as medical records, legal documents, and police reports, past criminal history, history of substance abuse, academic records, psychological test results and third party interviews should be considered when determining malingering IST.

In additional ruling out somatoform and factitious disorders is warranted when ruling out malingering. A Factitious disorder has no external incentive and the motivation is a psychological need to assume a sick role. Additional Factitious Disorders also present with symptoms that are consciously generated; thus intentionally feigned. Factitious Disorders and Malingering share this feature. On the other hand, Somatoform Disorders typically present with symptoms that are unconsciously generated; thus that they are not intentionally feigned.

Furthermore, Somatoform Disorder external incentive and motivation may include attention, financial compensation, avoiding stressful situations or to avoid arrest; both malingering and Somatoform Disorder share this feature.

DIFFERENTIAL DIAGNOSIS IN MALINGERING

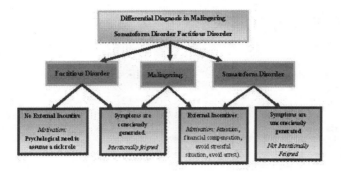

Chapter Ten

Summarizing the Detection of Malingering

Detecting malingering can be a difficult task for the forensic psychologist. False positives; the reason for poor performance or effort may vary from person to person depending on the evaluee's overall biopsychosocial makeup, IQ, maturity, age, overall physiological, emotional, psychological, and cognitive development, and motivation (if any) of the defendant to malinger can all play a role in whether the evaluee will attempt malingering; or is perceived to be malingering.

Furthermore, the clinician should rule out other potential conditions where malingering is a symptom which causes feigning; such as Factitious Disorders; attention seeking personality disorders, such as Histrionic Personality Disorder; Munchausen Syndrome by Proxy; Narcissistic Personality Disorder and Somatoform Disorders) (DSM-IV-TR, 2000).

The clinician should be cognizant of inconsistencies or exaggerations during the evaluation. Additionally, careful observation of verbal and nonverbal cues, behaviors, and body language of the evaluee should also be assessed during the forensic psychological exam and evaluation. Moreover, the delivery of psychological instruments, the type of psychological instrument used, in addition to cultural factors when choosing a psychological instrument should be considered. Finally, an objective, nonjudgmental, unbiased interpretation of test results; in addition to the previously mentioned criteria and assessment technique and individual characteristics/circumstances of the client/evlauee will all play a role in the outcome of whether a defendant is "deemed" incompetent to stand trial.

References

Acklin, M. (2010) *Forensic Clinician's Tool Box: Competency to Stand Trial measures*. Retrieved on July 19, 2011 from

Adetunji, B., Basil, B., Mathews, M., Williams, A., Osinowo, T., Oladinni, O. (2006) Detection and Management of Malingering in a Clinical Setting. P*rimary Psychiatry.* 2006;13(1):61-69

American Psychiatric Association (2000). Diagnostic and Statistical Manual of Mental Disorders (4th ed.) Test Revision. Washington DC. APA

American Psychological Association (1991). *Specialty Guidelines for Forensic Psychology* (Draft 2.0 of 2-13-05) American Psychological Association, and American Board of Forensic Psychology

American Psychological Association (2001). *Ethical Principles of Psychologists and Code of Conduct 2010 Amendments*

Bagby, R. M., Rogers, R., Nicholson, R., Buis, T., Seeman, M. V., & Rector, N. (1997).
Does clinical training facilitate feigning schizophrenia on the MMPI-2? *Psychological Assessment, 9,* 106-112.

Bordinia, E., Chaknisb, M., Ekman-Turnerc, R., Pernad, R. (2002). Advances and issues in the diagnostic differential of malingering versus brain injury. *Neuro-Rehabilitation* 17 93-104. IOS Press.

Buchanan, A. (2006) Competency to Stand Trial and the Seriousness of the Charge. The Journal of the American Academy of Psychiatry and the Law, 34 (4), 458-465. Retieved on July 21, 2011 from Proquest database

Bush, S.S., Connell, M.A., & Denney, R.L. (in press). Ethical Decision-Making Model. APA Books. *Ethical Issues in Forensic Psychology* Competency to Stand Trial-Assessment Instrument.

Elkins, J. (2010) *Criminal Law: Competency to Stand Trial.*

Felthous, A. (2011). Competence to Stand Trial Should Require Rational Understanding. The *Journal of American Academy of Psychiatry and the Law*, 39 (1), 19-30.

Fitzpatrick, M. (2006) Department of Justice Study: Mental Illness of Prison Inmates Worse Than Past Estimates: Reflects Failures in Mental Healthcare System

Gacono CB, Meloy JR, Sheppard K, Speth E, Roske A.A clinical investigation of malingering and psychopathy in hospitalized insanity acquittees. Am Acad Psychiatry Law. 1995;23(3):387-97.

Giger, P., Merten, T., Merkelbach, H., Oswald, M. (2010) Detection of Feigned Crime-Related Amnesia: A Multi-Method Approach. *Journal of Forensic Psychology Practice*, 10:440–463, 2010. DOI: 10.1080/15228932.2010.489875

Gordon, R. (2011). Definitions of MMPI/MMPI-2 scales: Scales of Validity and Bias.

Iverson, G. (2006) Ethical Issues Associated With the Assessment of Exaggeration, Poor Effort, and Malingering. *Applied Neuropsychology*, 13 (2), 77-90.

John Jay College of Criminal Justice

Kucharski, T., Falkenbach, D., Egan, S., Ducan, S. (2006). Antisocial Personality Disorder and the Malingering of Psychiatric Disorder: A Study of Criminal Defendants. *International Journal of Forensic Mental Health,* 5 (2), 195-204

Melton, G., Petrila, J., Poythress,N., Slobogin, C. (2007). *Psychological Evaluations for the Courts: A Handbook for Mental Health Professionals and Lawyers* (3rd ed.) New York: Guilford Press.

Oorsouw, K., Merckelbach, H. (2010) Detecting malingered memory problems in the civil and criminal arena. *Legal and Criminological Psychology*, 15. 97-114 *The British Psychological Society*

Pirelli, G., Gottdiener, W., Zaf, P. (2011). A Meta-Analytic Review of Competency to Stand Trial Research. Psychology, Public Policy, and Law, 17 (1) 1-53. American Psychological Association

Psychologyadvice.com. (2011). What Do We Know About Psychopathy? Do certain psychological traits predispose people to criminal behavior?

Roesch, R., Zaqpf, P., Golding,S., Skeem, J., (2004), Defining and Assessing Competency to Stand Trial

Rogers, R., Johansson-Love, J. (2009) Evaluating Competency to Stand Trial with Evidence-Based Practice. *Journal Am Acad Psychiatry Law* **37**:450–60, 2009

Rogers, R. Jackson, R., Sewell, K., Harrison, K (2004). An Examination of the ECST-R as a Screen for Feigned Incompetency to Stand Trial. *American Psychological Association* 16, No. 2, 139–145 DOI: 10.1037/1040-3590.16.2.139

Rubenzer, S. (2011). Review of the Inventory of Legal Knowledge. Open Access Journal of Forensic Psychology, 3(11).

Teichner, G., Wagner, M. (2004) The Test of Memory Malingering (TOMM): normative data from cognitively intact, cognitively impaired, and elderly patients with dementia.Archives of Clinical Neuropsychology 19 (2004) 455–464

United States Constitution; Amendment text. ET

Vitacco, M., Rogers, R., Gabel, J., Munizza, J. (2006). An Evaluation of Malingering Screens with Competency to Stand Trial Patients: A Known-Groups Comparison. American Psychology-Law Society . American Psychological Association

Wettstein, R. Ethics and Forensic Psychiatry

Made in United States
Orlando, FL
03 November 2023

38548272R00039